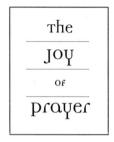

The
JOY
of
prayer

Volumes in the Pathway to the Heart of God series

The Experience of Prayer
The Journey of Prayer
The Joy of Prayer
A Time for Prayer

PATHWAY TO THE HEART OF GOD

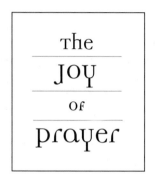

The
JOY
of
prayer

TERRY W. GLASPEY

Cumberland House Publishing
Nashville, Tennessee

Published by Cumberland House Publishing, Inc., 431 Harding Industrial Drive, Nashville, Tennessee 37211

Unless otherwise indicated, verses are taken from the Holy Bible, New International Version®, Copyright © 1973, 1978, 1984 by the International Bible Society. Used by permission of Zondervan Publishing House. The "NIV" and "New International Version" trademarks are registered in the United States Patent and Trademark Office by the International Bible Society.

Verses marked NASB are taken from the New American Standard Bible, © 1960, 1962, 1963, 1968, 1971, 1972, 1973, 1975, 1977 by The Lockman Foundation. Used by permission.

Cover design by Karen Phillips
Text design by Julia M. Pitkin

Library of Congress Cataloging-in-Publication Data

Glaspey, Terry W.
    The joy of prayer / Terry W. Glaspey
        p. cm. -- (Pathway to the heart of God series)
    ISBN 1-58182-133-6 (hardcover : alk. paper)
    1. Prayer. I. Title.

  BV210.2 .G588 2000
  248.3'2--dc21   00-057065

Printed in the United States of America
1 2 3 4 5 6 7 8 — 05 04 03 02 01 00

contents

introduction

What do people mean when they speak of prayer? Do they mean the act of asking God to do something for them—rescuing them from a dire circumstance or meeting a need or desire? Are they speaking of confession, of opening their heart in repentance for a thought, action, or word that hurts others? Or is it the giving of praise to God for His mercy and grace?

Of course, prayer is all these things and more. There are an amazing variety of uses to be found in prayer. The many different kinds of prayer reflect the different needs in our lives and demonstrate that there is a form of prayer adequate to every need, desire, and emotion. I invite you to join with the great Christian writers sampled here in experimenting with all the wondrous forms that prayer takes. Each is a different road to a single destination: a closer relationship with God.

The little book you hold in your hand is the second of four little books about prayer. This particular volume will focus on examining the different elements that go into creating a balanced and well-rounded life of prayer. The other books in the series look at what prayer really is and how God uses it so powerfully in our lives (*A Time for Prayer*), wrestle with some of the tough questions about prayer (*The Journey of Prayer*), and provide practical steps for beginning to make prayer a more integral part of our lives (*The Experience of Prayer*). Each of the four books is a part of the whole. Taken together, their goal is not only to help us understand prayer a little better, but also to inspire us to begin to pray.

Prayer is a topic that continues to be much discussed these days, especially by those who are concerned with making sense of their spiritual lives. There are lots of books around that attempt to explain the ins and outs of what prayer is and how it affects one's life. Some of them claim to have all the answers, to have unlocked some secret key or system for making prayer effective for the reader.

I make no such claim. Like you, I am a learner in the school of prayer. But one of the important things I have learned is that I am not on my own when it comes to making sense of this crucial element of my spiritual life. Many great thinkers, writers, theologians, mystics, and activists have ruminated deeply on this important topic. In this book, I hope to share a little of what I've learned from them, mostly in their own words. If, like me, you realize you have a lot to learn and you truly desire to make your prayer life more meaningful, then I invite you to join me in meditating on some of the most profound and life-changing words ever written about prayer.

Each year brings a multitude of new books on prayer. One of the lessons I have learned about such books is that the most recent ones are not necessarily the best ones. It seems that a lot of books published these days are tainted with our modern materialistic values or our current obsession with the therapeutic sphere. Such books tend to be more concerned with using prayer as a way to get what we want or as a method for obtaining inner peace and tranquility than with learning how to make communication with God a part of our honest everyday existence and with growing into a more intimate relationship with Him.

I invite you, then, to join me on a journey that will sample the thoughts of some of the most insightful believers who ever lived (along with a handful of unbelievers who thought deeply about the subject). These nuggets of wisdom are best absorbed thoughtfully and slowly, a few at a time. If we are to enter the school of prayer, we must not rush to consider ourselves graduates. Savor these thoughts. Meditate on them. Argue with them. Make them your own.

The writers quoted in this book come from a variety of time periods, religious traditions, cultures, and life experiences. Be forewarned: They do not always agree with each other. Most of the time I have simply allowed their disagreements to stand, expecting the reader to ponder their thoughts with discernment and draw his or her own conclusions. At other times, I have tried to synthesize the various insights together, still endeavoring to avoid the temptation of superficially explaining away the mysteries that will always surround this topic.

Sprinkled in with the text you'll also find some of my favorite prayers from classic writers, many of them composed by the same writers whose thoughts on prayer we will consider. You can use these prayers as models to fashion your own, as inspiration to prepare your heart to pray, or as a way to give voice to concerns and feelings you cannot articulate as well as these saints. You and I can make these prayers our own, for often they can help us express what we would struggle to put into words for ourselves. When prayed with focus and concentration, they can give our hearts wings to fly upward to God.

Finally, I have concluded each section of this book with a prayer I have written. These little prayers are attempts to put the truths of the chapter into practice...for it does us little good to think about prayer or read about praying if we don't actually pray.

I hope you will find this little book to be a helpful companion as you travel your own spiritual path. Think of it as a map you can use as you begin your personal journey into God's heart.

—Terry W. Glaspey

the

JOY

of

prayer

$-$I$-$

THE MANY ELEMENTS
OF PRAYER

One of the truths that struck me most powerfully as I undertook my own study of prayer from the Scriptures and the great Christian writers was the incredible variety there is in the life of prayer. There is a tendency for us to see prayer in a narrow and limited way. When we hear the word *prayer,* our mind jumps to one or two different kinds of prayer, failing to understand that prayer encompasses so many different aspects of our walk with God.

When we look closely at the topic of prayer, we find that there are several different elements of prayer, each aimed at a particular need in our lives. The classic writers remind us that each of these kinds of prayer is necessary for a balanced life of communion with God. Some have tried to quantify them:

> *The principal parts of prayer*
> *are Invocation with Adoration, Confession,*
> *Petition, Intercession with Thanksgiving.*
> —PHILIP DODDRIDGE

Doddridge's list of "principal parts" seems to encompass the major elements in the life of prayer. A little acrostic I learned years ago in Sunday school makes them easy to remember. Perhaps you're familiar with it too:

> A–Adoration
> C–Confession
> T–Thanksgiving
> S–Supplication

One well-known early church writer and theologian, Origen, went into great detail to explain these four key elements of the life of prayer:

> *It seems to me there are four topics that*
> *need to be sketched out and that I have found*
> *scattered in the Scriptures, indicating that each*
> *one should organize one's prayer according*
> *to these topics. This is what they are: In the*
> *beginning and the preface of the prayer*

*something having the force of praise should
be said of God through Christ, who is
praised with Him, and by the Holy Spirit,
who is hymned with Him, After this each person
should place general thanksgivings, bringing
forward for thanksgiving the benefits given
many people and those he has himself received
from God. After thanksgiving it seems to me
that he ought to blame himself bitterly before
God for his own sins and then ask, first,
for healing that he may be delivered from
the habit that brings him to sin and, second,
for forgiveness of the sins that have been
committed. And after confession, the fourth
topic that seems to me must be added is
the request for great and heavenly things,
both private and general, and concerning
his household and his dearest. And, finally,
the prayer should be concluded with a doxology
of God through Christ in the Holy Spirit.*

*First, giving praise may be found
in the following words from Psalm 104:1-3:
"O Lord my God, Thou art great indeed,
clothed with majesty and splendor, and
wrapped in a robe of light. Thou hast
spread out the heavens like a tent and*

*on their waters laid the beams of Thy
pavilion; who takest the clouds for Thy
chariot, riding on the wings of the wind."*

*As for thanksgiving...David is amazed
at God's gifts and thanks Him for them in
these words, "What am I, LORD God, and
what is my family, that Thou hast brought
me thus far?"—2 Samuel 7:18.*

*An example of confession is: "My wounds
fester and stink because of my folly. I am
bowed down and utterly prostrate. All day
long I go about as if in mourning"—Psalm 38.5-6.*

*An example of petition or request
is found in Psalm 28.3: "Do not drag me away
with the ungodly, with evildoers." Other
examples are like this one.*

*And having begun with praise it is right
to conclude the prayer by ending with praise,
hymning and glorifying the Father of all through
Jesus Christ in the Holy Spirit, to whom be glory
forever—cf. Romans 16:27; Hebrews 13:21;
Galatians 1:5; 2 Timothy 4:18.*
                    —ORIGEN

If our prayers fail to take into account all these various elements of prayer, then we have robbed ourselves of many of the joys and much of the power of praying. If we only know and practice one kind of prayer, then we have placed a limitation on the rich variety of circumstances where prayer can connect us with God's bountiful goodness.

Some may come to God only in times of crisis, calling out for help for specific needs. Others may only when they are motivated by a sense of guilt. Some may be quick to thank God, but slow to feel secure in asking anything of Him. Still others will find it reasonable to offer praise to the One who is the creator of all things, but not feel confident that His concern for His creation extends even to the small things in our personal lives.

It is not until we grasp the incredible variety of elements in prayer that we can be bold to come to God in every circumstance with every feeling, desire, and need.

Thank you Father,
for the gift of prayer.
For a way to reach out to you.
A way deeper than our human means.
Thank you for all the various elements of prayer,
each of them a way by which we may
draw closer to you.
In Jesus we pray,
Amen.

2

ADORATION: LIfTING OUR HEART TO GOD

What is our natural response when we see a painting so marvelously crafted that it speaks to something deep within us? Or when we hear a musical performance whose virtuosity takes our breath away? Or when we witness a display of athletic prowess that seems to transcend human limitations? Is it not our natural human response to speak with awe and wonder of the marvels we have seen, to lift up our voice and testify of their surpassing greatness?

Is it not also very natural for us to speak of our love to those whom we care deeply about? What relationship would be considered healthy where there was no verbal communication of care, concern, appreciation, and depth of love? It does not seem right to us that our deepest feelings should go unspoken.

When our hearts overflow with affection or admiration, we seem to need to put words to our feelings. It should not only be this way in our relationships with those around us, but also in our relationship with God. We should tell Him how we feel, and honor Him for who He is. For what is greater than the wonder of His power, more heart-stirring than the beauty of His creation, more glorious than His holiness? To whom could we possibly owe more than we owe to Him?

There is certainly no more important element of prayer than adoration, the rendering of praise to God for who He is. Until we recognize both His greatness and our need for Him, we have little hope of meaningful prayer.

To do so at the outset of our prayer sets up the proper relationship between God and ourselves.

Upon offering this sacrifice of praise,
the heart is further enlarged to pray
for fresh blessings. We are never fitter
to pray than after praise.
—RICHARD SIBBES

A great part of my time is spent
in getting my heart in tune for prayer. It is the
divine link that connects earth with heaven.
—ROBERT MURRAY MCCHEYNE

Here is the secret of a life of prayer.
Take time in the inner chamber to bow down
and worship; and wait on Him until He unveils
Himself, and takes possession of you, and goes out
with you to show how a man can live and walk
in abiding fellowship with an unseen Lord.
—ANDREW MURRAY

*God cannot hear the prayers on our lips
often because the desires of our heart after the
world cry out to Him much more strongly
and loudly than our desires for Him.*
—ANDREW MURRAY

There is no better use of the human tongue than
to offer praise and worship to God.

*Ascribe to the LORD the glory due his name.
Bring an offering and come before him; worship
the LORD in the splendor of his holiness.*
—I CHRONICLES 16:29

The best atmosphere for prayer is praise.
—PETER ANDERSON

0 God, you are my God,
earnestly I seek you; my soul thirsts for you,
my body longs for you, in a dry and weary land
where there is no water. I have seen you in the
sanctuary and beheld your power and your
glory. Because your love is better than life,
my lips will glorify you. I will praise you
as long as I live, and in your name
I will lift up my hands.
—PSALM 63:1-4

All true prayer is worship—the ascription
of worth to the Eternal. Without adoration,
thanksgiving may become a miserliness, petition
a selfish clamor, intercession a currying of special
favors for our friends, and even contemplation
may turn into a refined indulgence.
—GEORGE BUTTRICK

Receive every day as a resurrection
from death, as a new enjoyment of life;
meet every rising sun with such sentiments
of God's goodness, as if you had seen it, and
all things, new created on your account: and
under the sense of so great a blessing, let
your joyful heart praise and magnify
so good and glorious a Creator.
—WILLIAM LAW

The end we ought to propose
to ourselves is to become, in this life,
the most perfect worshippers of God we
can possibly be, as we hope to
be through all eternity.
—BROTHER LAWRENCE

Our father,
if it is our destiny to offer praise to you forever,
what could be more seemly than
that we begin now
to practice what will be our eternal occupation.
And yet, your greatness is such
That all the words we could speak
from now until eternity
would be inadequate to sum up
the majesty of your glory.
still we offer our humble praise
for who you are and what you have done.
Amen.

3

CONFESSION: OPENING
OUR HEART TO GOD

Sometimes we are hesitant to come before God in prayer because of the state of our hearts or lives. And it is appropriate that we feel some hesitation, for there is a natural sense of shame that overcomes us when we realize that we live out our lives before the all-seeing eyes of God. Our actions, of course, are witnessed by Him, but even our thoughts are transparent to the One who made us. And in the brightness of God's holiness, all our imperfections and evasions become clear. The darkness of our own self-deceptions must flee in the dawning of His light. We see ourselves as we really are, and sometimes that is not a pleasant experience.

If we honestly examine ourselves—our actions, our attitudes, even our motivations—we will find that we fall short; there is much within us that is contrary to the spirit of Christ who dwells within. This being the case, it would be unseemly to come to God with our mouths full of requests while our hearts are filled with self-righteousness, evil imaginations, bitter emotions, and self-serving attitudes. These must be cleansed from us as we enter His presence.

We should not come before God lightly. To approach a holy God, we must be cleansed and purified in our hearts. But this cleansing cannot come about through our own efforts. If the only result of realizing our sinfulness is to make us feel guilty, then our awareness profits us little. For God wipes away sin when we confess it and accept the forgiveness He offers. Therefore, confession of sin is an absolutely essential ingredient in our prayer as it is the act that shows how serious we are about wanting God to intervene in our lives.

*Before all else, let us list sincere thanksgiving
first on the scroll of our prayer. On the second line,
we should put confession and heartfelt contrition
of soul. Then let us present our petition to the
King of all. This is the best way of prayer.*
—JOHN CLIMACUS

*Come near to God and he will come near to you.
Wash your hands, you sinners, and purify your
hearts, you double-minded.*
—JAMES 4:8

*Until known sin is judged and renounced,
we pray and plead in vain.*
—OSWALD CHAMBERS

No man may come to God,
but upon his knees. I speak not of the bowing
of the knee, but of the heart.
—RICHARD SIBBES

Our offenses are many in your sight,
and our sins testify against us. Our offenses
are ever with us, and we acknowledge our iniquities:
rebellion and treachery against the LORD, turning our
backs on our God, fomenting oppression and revolt,
uttering lies our hearts have conceived.
—ISAIAH 59:12,13

You know my folly, O God;
my guilt is not hidden from you.
—PSALM 69:5

Let us examine our ways and test them,
and let us return to the LORD.
—LAMENTATIONS 3:40

Wounds cannot be healed until they
are revealed and sins cannot be forgiven
until they are confessed.
—MARTIN LUTHER

True confession is not merely mental assent that we have done wrong. It means opening our heart to God and allowing ourselves to feel deep sorrow for our misdeeds and the attitudes of our hearts.

*A prayer without penitence
is a prayer without acceptance. If no
tear has fallen upon it, it is withered. There
must be confession of sin before God,
or our prayer is faulty.*
—CHARLES SPURGEON

*Whoever wishes to advance in building up virtue
will do so through weeping and tears.*
—ABBA ANTHONY

*Content not yourself with confessing your…sins,
merely as to the fact, but accuse yourself also of
the motive that induced you to commit them.*
—FRANCIS DE SALES

*The fire of sin is intense, but it is put out by
a small amount of tears, for the tear puts out a
furnace of faults, and cleans our wounds of sin.*
—JOHN CHRYSOSTOM

*Through the Prayer of Tears
we give God permission to show us
our sinfulness and the sinfulness of
the world at the emotional level.*
—RICHARD FOSTER

*If you have ever been under trial
before an earthly judge, you will not need
any other pattern for your attitude in prayer.
But if you have never stood before a judge yourself
and have not seen others being cross-questioned,
then learn at least from the way the sick implore
the surgeons when they are about to be
operated on or cauterized.*
—JOHN CLIMACUS

One of the sins we must confess to God, lest
it hinder our prayer, is any animosity we hold
against others. A heart filled with bitterness is a
heart that has no room to receive forgiveness.

*For what sort of deed is it
to approach the God of peace
without peace, or to ask for the remission
of debts while you retain them? How will he
appease his Father who is angry with his brother....
Even if we must be angry, our anger must not be
maintained beyond sunset, as the apostle admon-
ishes....Nor merely from anger, but altogether from all
perturbation of mind, ought the exercise of prayer to
be free, uttered from a spirit such as the Spirit unto
whom it is sent. For a defiled spirit cannot be
acknowledged by a holy Spirit, nor a sad
by a joyful, nor a fettered by a free.*
—TERTULLIAN

*If you forgive men when they sin
against you, your heavenly Father will also
forgive you. But if you do not forgive men their
sins, your Father will not forgive your sins.*
—MATTHEW 6:14, 15

The end result of confession is the knowledge that we are forgiven. This knowledge has two aspects: an intellectual awareness and an existential awareness. The forgiveness that God offers in Christ is an intellectual assurance. It is a truth we can know beyond a shadow of a doubt. We are forgiven even when we do not feel forgiven. It is a reality based upon what He has done, His free choice.

Paradoxically, however, there is an existential element as well. When we know that God has forgiven us, we will often experience that truth as a liberating emotion. We feel a great burden and weight lifted from our souls. We are made free from the tyranny of sin and given the opportunity to "start over." Again and again, God gives us the ability to reaffirm our commitment to Him and to start anew, with a clean slate, because He has forgiven our sin.

But forgiveness begins with asking.

If we confess our sins,
he is faithful and just and will
forgive us our sins and purify us
from all unrighteousness.
—1 JOHN 1:9

When I kept silent about my sin,
my body wasted away through my
groaning all day long. For day and night
Thy hand was heavy upon me; My vitality
was drained away as with the fever heat of
summer. I acknowledged my sin to Thee,
And my iniquity I did not hide; I said,
"I will confess my transgressions to
the LORD." And Thou didst
forgive the guilt of my sin.
—PSALM 32:3-5, NASB

He who conceals his sins
does not prosper, but whoever confesses
and renounces them finds mercy
—PROVERBS 28:13

The first characteristic of the
kingdom of heaven is the overflowing joy
that comes from contrition and repentance.
—BASILEA SCHLINK

The confession of evil works
is the first beginning of good works.
—AUGUSTINE

So, let us join with David in baring our souls
before God, that He might make us clean.

Have mercy on me, O God,
according to your unfailing love, according to
your great compassion blot out my transgressions.
Wash away all my iniquity and
cleanse me from my sin.

For I know my transgressions,
and my sin is always before me.
Against you, you only, have I sinned
and done what is evil in your sight....

Create in me a pure heart, O God,
and renew a steadfast spirit within me.
Do not cast me from your presence or take
your Holy Spirit from me. Restore to me
the joy of your salvation and grant me
a willing spirit, to sustain me.
—PSALM 51:1-4, 10-12

Heavenly Father,
awaken within me a sense of the
magnitude of my sin.
Teach me not to justify it;
not to excuse it because of circumstances;
not to treat it lightly nor underestimate
its impact,
awaken within me a trust in the
magnitude of your power.
your ability to change me;
to transform me;
to make me a new creature by the
strength of your forgiveness.
In Jesus' name,
amen.

4

THANKSGIVING: EXPRESSING OUR APPRECIATION

One of the strongest motivations to prayer is our gratitude for who God is and what He has accomplished for us. Our hearts should be thankful as we come before Him.

To have a thankful heart changes our attitudes. Even when our circumstances do not change, thankfulness changes the way we view those circumstances. It reminds us of the sovereignty of God and helps us to remember that truly "all things work together for good" (Romans 8:28). Behind the scenes, an unseen hand is shaping us by shaping the events of our lives.

Thankfulness can arise when we remember the way that God's providence has led us in the past.

Sometimes it's hard to understand what is happening when we are in the midst of trying times, but in retrospect we are usually able to see how God's good hand has guided us. When we thank God for His past works, it helps us muster the confidence we need in our present darkness and look toward His future providence in our lives.

When we realize that everything good in our lives comes from His hand, our only proper response is to be grateful.

To pray is to regain a sense of the mystery that animates all beings, the divine margin in all attainments. Prayer is our humble answer to the inconceivable surprise of living. It is all we can offer in return for the mystery by which we live. Who is worthy to be present at the constant unfolding of time? Amidst the meditation of mountains, the humility of flowers—wiser than all the alphabets—clouds that die constantly for the sake of His glory, we are hating, hunting, hurting. Suddenly we feel ashamed of our clashes and complaints in the face of the tacit glory in nature. It is so embarrassing to live! How strange we are in the world, and how presumptuous our doings! Only one response can maintain us: gratefulness for witnessing the wonder, for the gift of our unearned right to serve, to adore, and to fulfill. It is gratefulness which makes the soul great.
—ABRAHAM HESCHEL

Devote yourselves to prayer,
being watchful and thankful.
—COLOSSIANS 4:2

Give thanks to the LORD,
call on his name, make known among
the nations what he has done.
—I CHRONICLES 16:8

Let the peace of Christ rule in your hearts,
since as members of one body you were called
to peace. And be thankful.
—COLOSSIANS 3:15

*Since we are receiving a kingdom that cannot
be shaken, let us be thankful, and so worship
God acceptably with reverence and awe.*
—HEBREWS 12:28

*Always [give] thanks to God the Father
for everything, in the name of our
Lord Jesus Christ.*
—EPHESIANS 5:20

*Give thanks to the Lord, for he is good;
his love endures forever.*
—PSALM 107:1

*O Lord! that lends me life,
Lend me a heart replete with thankfulness!*
—WILLIAM SHAKESPEARE

When all is going well, we find it easy to give thanks. We are always ready to give thanks when our circumstances are positive. But what about the times when life isn't going so well? Sometimes our hurts and struggles seem to choke down our desire to give thanks. We struggle, wondering how we can appreciate circumstances that are painful. But the catalyst that will give voice to thanksgiving is the realization that our lives are a great gift from one whose concern is beyond our momentary pleasures and who wishes to impart eternal delights.

Though it can be hard to do so, we need to be thankful even when it seems there is very little reason for thankfulness. Only then do we show that we have fully placed our trust in God.

Do not be anxious about anything, but in everything,
by prayer and petition, with thanksgiving, present
your requests to God.
—PHILIPPIANS 4:6

It is easy to sing when we can read
the notes by daylight; but he is skillful who
sings when there is not a ray of light to read by—
who sings from his heart....It is not in man's power
to sing when all is adverse, unless an altar-coal
shall touch his lip....O Thou chief musician,
let us not remain songless because affliction
is upon us, but tune Thou our lips to
the melody of thanksgiving.
—CHARLES SPURGEON

Thankfulness is not only an element of prayer;
it will also be the end result of prayer: From prayer
to praise is never a long or difficult journey.
—CHARLES SPURGEON

Lord,
my heart is full of thanks to you.
For the little things and the great.
For the revelations of your glory
and the moments of doubt.
For joy in abundance and security
in times of need.
For life, for friends, for family.
For healing and hope.
For everything you have done for me.
But mostly, Lord, I am thankful
for who you are.
A god of awesome holiness and
incomprehensible power
who is my creator, redeemer, sustainer,
companion, and friend.
Amen.

5

SUPPLICATION: MAKING
OUR NEEDS KNOWN

We all have many wants and needs in our lives.
We have hopes and dreams, desires and passionate
longings. And though we know from Scripture
that God loves and cares for us, we sometimes are
reluctant to share our concerns with Him because
we fear that they're not important enough. In the
grand scheme of things, some of our concerns may
seem trivial, even to us—they seem much too
small for God to be bothered with. And so, sometimes we keep our needs to ourselves.

But we must never think that it is somehow
more spiritual to suffer quietly, with only the assistance of our own resources, than to bring our
needs and concerns before God. For He not only
wants to give us the gift of eternal life, but also to
provide us with what we need in our day-to-day

earthly existence. It is our pride that sometimes stands in the way. We must admit that we need God. We need His involvement in our lives if we are to live them to the fullest. We should feel free, then, to ask God to supply our daily needs.

*Whether we like it or not, asking
is the rule of the Kingdom.*
—CHARLES SPURGEON

*It is men's ignorance of themselves
that makes prayer little in request: hunger
best teaches men to beg. You would be oftener
on your knees, if you were oftener in your hearts.
Prayer would not seem so needless, if you
knew your needs. Know yourselves,
and be prayerless if you can.*
—UNKNOWN

*Prayer is not conquering
God's reluctance, but taking hold
of God's willingness.*
—PHILLIPS BROOKS

Prayer covers the whole of a man's life.
There is no thought, feeling, yearning, or desire,
however low, trifling, or vulgar we may deem it,
which, if it affects our interest or happiness, we
may not lay before God and be sure of sympathy.
His nature is such that our often coming does not
tire Him. The whole burden of the whole life of
every man may be rolled on to God and not
weary Him, though it has wearied the man.
—HENRY WARD BEECHER

As many turn to a good and generous
man because they hope to obtain from him
what they need, so those who have a firm,
untroubled trust in God, rich in charity and
generosity, beg from him pardon and assistance.
Prayer is a request for something good,
addressed to God by pious men.
—TIKHON OF ZADONSK

Is any one of you in trouble? He should pray.
—JAMES 5:13

In my distress I called to the LORD;
I cried to my God for help. From his temple
he heard my voice; my cry came
before him, into his ears.
—PSALM 18:6

In the day of my trouble I will call to you,
for you will answer me.
—PSALM 86:7

If we will make use of prayer,
not to wrest from God advantages
for ourselves or our dear ones, or to escape
from tribulations and difficulties, but to call
down upon ourselves and others those things
which will glorify the name of God, then we
shall see the strongest and boldest promises
of the Bible about prayer fulfilled also
in our weak, little prayer life.
—O. HALLESBY

For when you mention and pray
for daily bread, you pray for everything
that is necessary in order to have and enjoy
daily bread and, on the other hand, against
everything which interferes with it. Therefore you
must open wide and extend your thoughts not
only to the oven or the flour-bin but to the distant
field and the entire land, which bears and brings
to us daily bread and every sort of sustenance.
For if God did not cause it to grow, and bless
and preserve it in the field, we could never
take bread from the oven or have
any to set upon the table.
—MARTIN LUTHER

Dealing in generalities is the death of prayer.
—J. H. EVANS

*Any concern too small to be
turned into a prayer is too small
to be made into a burden,*
—CORRIE TEN BOOM

*Desires and longings are the essence
of supplication, and it little matters what
shape they take. "O that" is as acceptable
a prayer as "Our Father."*
—CHARLES SPURGEON

*Prayer is not designed for
the furnishing of God with the knowledge
of what we need, but it is designed as a
confession to Him of our sense of need.*
—A.W. PINK

If we want to describe our prayers,
they are really nothing more than the
stammering of children who ask for bread
or a morsel before meals. For we do not know
what we should ask for. The things we ask for are
beyond our comprehension, and He who bestows
them is greater; and the things are also too great
for our narrow hearts to be able to understand.
—MARTIN LUTHER

We can boldly ask God to meet our needs
because of the many promises that He has made in
the Scriptures. It is not presumptuous to ask Him
for what has already been offered.

The promise is the bow
by which we shoot the arrows
of supplication.
—CHARLES SPURGEON

*I could go from one end of the Bible
to the other, and produce an astonishing
variety of texts that are applicable as promises;
enough to prove, that in whatever circumstances
a child of God may be placed, God has provided
in the Bible some promise, either general or
particular, which He can apply, that
is precisely suited to his case.*
—CHARLES G. FINNEY

*We must be concerned with the
person and character of God, not
the promises. Through the promises we
learn what God has willed to us, we learn
what we may claim as our heritage, we learn
how we should pray. But faith itself
must rest on the character of God,*
—A.W. TOZER

Prayer takes the promise to the bank of faith,
and obtains the golden blessing.
—CHARLES SPURGEON

When we make our needs known to God, then, we should ask with earnestness in our hearts, coming in boldness before the heavenly Father. All the passion within our souls should be released in the act of prayer.

Supplication, in which a man's proper self
is not thoroughly present in agonizing earnestness
and vehement desire, is utterly ineffectual.
—CHARLES SPURGEON

*To pray…is to desire; but it is
to desire what God would have us desire.
He who desires not from the bottom of his
heart, offers a deceitful prayer.*
—FRANÇOIS FÉNELON

We should also never make the mistake of thinking that biblical prayer is merely polite request.
Sometimes it is appropriate that we plead with
God, that we ask and keep on asking. Some of the
great writers on prayer have referred to this as
"prevailing prayer."

*He [Jesus] said to them, "Suppose one of you
has a friend, and he goes to him at midnight and
says, 'Friend, lend me three loaves of bread, because
a friend of mine on a journey has come to me, and
I have nothing to set before him.'*

*"Then the one inside answers, 'Don't bother
me. The door is already locked, and my children
are with me in bed. I can't get up and give you
anything.' I tell you, though he will not get up
and give him the bread because he is his friend,
yet because of the man's boldness he will get up
and give him as much as he needs.*

*"So I say to you: Ask, and it will be given to you;
seek and you will find; knock and the door will be
opened to you. For everyone who asks receives;
he who seeks finds; and to him who knocks,
the door will be opened."*

—LUKE 11:5-10

Plead with God; plead with God;
plead with God! That praying is poor shift
that is not made up of pleading. "Bring forth
your reasons," saith the Lord. Bring forth your
strong arguments. O, what prayers were those
of John Knox, when he seemed to say to God,
"Save Scotland for this reason—for that reason—
for another reason—for yet one more reason"
—the number of his motives still multiplying
with the fervor of his heart. So did he labor
with God as though he pleaded for his life,
and would not let Him go until he had
gained his suit for Scotland.
—CHARLES SPURGEON

Men only pray with prevailing prayer who do so
amid the sobs and sighing of the race.
—G. CAMPBELL MORGAN

Lose the importunity of prayer,
reduce it to soliloquy, or even to colloquy,
with God, lose the real conflict of will, lose
the habit of wrestling and the hope of prevailing
with God, make it mere walking with God in
friendly talk, and, precious as that is, yet you
tend to lose the reality of prayer at last.
—P.T. FORSYTH

The great fault of the children of God is,
they do not continue in prayer; they do not
go on praying; they do not persevere. If they
desire anything for God's glory, they should
pray until they get it, Oh, how good, and kind,
and gracious, and condescending is the One
with Whom we have to do! He has given me,
unworthy as I am, immeasurably above
all I had asked or thought!
—GEORGE MUELLER

*Prayer is made vigorous by petitioning,
urgent by supplication; by thanksgiving,
pleasing and acceptable. Strength and acceptance
combine to prevail and secure the petition.*
—MARTIN LUTHER

*Prevailing prayer is often offered
in the present day, when Christians
have been wrought up to such a pitch
of importunity and such a holy boldness
that afterwards when they looked back
upon it, they were frightened and amazed at
themselves, to think they should have dared to
exercise such importunity with God. And yet
these prayers have prevailed, and obtained
the blessing. And many of these persons,
with whom I am acquainted, are among
the holiest persons I know in the world.*
—CHARLES G. FINNEY

*We must repeat the same supplications
not twice or three times only, but as often as we
have need, a hundred and a thousand times.*
—JOHN CALVIN

*Prayer is no fitful, short-lived thing.
It is no voice crying unheard and unheeded
in the silence. It is a voice which goes into God's
ear, and it lives as long as God's ear is open to
holy pleas, as long as God's heart is alive to holy
things. God shapes the world by prayer. Prayers are
deathless. The lips that utter them may be closed in
death, the heart that felt them may have ceased to
beat, but the prayers live before God, and God's
heart is set on them. Prayers outlive the lives of
those who uttered them; outlive a generation,
outlive an age, outlive a world.*
—E. M. BOUNDS

Biblical prayer is impertinent,
persistent, shameless, indecorous. It is
more like haggling in an outdoor bazaar
than the polite monologues of the churches.
—WALTER WINK

Of course, in all our asking, we must remember that God doesn't exist simply to serve our selfish wants. He is the heavenly Father, not a cosmic vending machine!

Prayer is often conceived to
be little more than a technique for
self-advancement, a heavenly method
for achieving earthly success.
—A. W. TOZER

God is not a cosmic bell-boy
for whom we can press a button
to get things.
—HARRY EMERSON FOSDICK

So then, prayer is a gift whereby we are offered
an open ear to all our concerns. God hears our
prayers and out of His love He concerns Himself
with what concerns us. But first we must be bold
enough to ask.

Heavenly Father,
Help us learn to be bold in our asking.
Realizing that it is your desire to meet our needs.
Help us learn to be persistent in our asking,
Realizing that you desire to wrestle
with us in prayer.
Help us learn to be wise in our asking,
Realizing that the power of prayer is in the
accomplishing of your will.
Help us learn the paradox that you,
the greatest giver
who gives so freely and richly,
so often want to be asked.
In christ,
Amen.

-6-

INTERCESSION: PRAYING FOR OTHERS

Many of us, when we pray, usually develop our prayers around a number of requests related to our own needs. We come into God's presence with a shopping list of what we would like Him to accomplish for us. Of course, as we saw in the last chapter, there is nothing wrong with bringing our personal petitions before God. We should do that. The problem arises when our prayers become so self-centered that we think only of our own needs.

Sometimes our requests command so much of our attention that we forget to pray for others. When we have desperate needs of our own, it is all too easy for us to forget that others have needs as well.

As we come before God with our requests, we must think not only of our own needs but also those of others, and we should lift them up before God. When we see others struggling, in pain or in want, our hearts are often moved to try to do something to help. Whenever we can do something to alleviate people's pain or meet their practical needs, it is our responsibility and privilege to do so. But sometimes there seems to be nothing we can do. We feel helpless.

Yet we need to remember that there is always something we can do for others—something powerful: We can pray for them. No matter how trite the phrase, "I'll pray for you" may sound sometimes, it is not a trite act when we follow through on our promise. Great power is unleashed when we address God on behalf of another person.

Pray in the Spirit on all occasions
with all kinds of prayers and requests
With this in mind, be alert and always
keep on praying for all the saints.
—EPHESIANS 6:18

I urge, then, first of all,
that requests, prayers, intercession and
thanksgiving be made for everyone.
—I TIMOTHY 2:I

Help us by your prayers. Then many will
give thanks on our behalf for the gracious favor
granted us in answer to the prayers of many.
—2 CORINTHIANS I:II

The thought of our fellowship in the intercession of Jesus reminds us of what He has taught us more than once before, how all these wonderful prayer-promises have as their aim and justification, the glory of God in the manifestation of His kingdom and the salvation of sinners. As long as we only or chiefly pray for ourselves, the promises of the last night must remain a sealed book to us. It is to the fruit-bearing branches of the Vine; it is to disciples sent into the world as the Father sent Him, to live for perishing men: it is to His faithful servants and intimate friends who take up the work He leaves behind, who have like their Lord become as the seed-corn, losing its life to multiply it manifold—it is to such that the promises are given. Let us each find out what the work is, and who the souls are entrusted to our special prayers; let us make our intercession for them our life of fellowship with God, and we shall not only find the promises of power in prayer made true to us, but we shall then first begin to realize how our abiding in Christ and His abiding in us make us share in His own joy of blessing and saving men.

—ANDREW MURRAY

Our prayer must not be self-centered.
It must arise not only because we feel our own
need as a burden which we must lay upon God,
but also because we are bound up in love for our
fellow men that we feel their need as acutely as
our own. To make intercession for men is the
most powerful and practical way in which
we can express our love for them.
—JOHN CALVIN

We are all selfish by nature
and our selfishness is very apt to stick to us,
even when we are converted. There is a tendency
in us to think only of our own needs, our own
spiritual conflicts, and our own progress
in religion and forget others.
—J.C. RYLE

*Intercessory prayer is the purifying bath
into which the individual and the fellowship
must enter every day.*
—DIETRICH BONHOEFFER

*Prayers for men are far more important
than prayers for things because men more
deeply concern God's will and the work
of Jesus Christ than things.*
—E.M. BOUNDS

*Necessity binds us to pray for ourselves,
fraternal charity urges us to pray for others:
and the prayer that fraternal charity proffers
is sweeter to God than that which is the
outcome of necessity.*
—JOHN CHRYSOSTOM

When we lift each other up in prayer, not only can God answer the need of our brother or sister, but He can also draw us closer to one another. In heartfelt intercession we find the depths of Christian love.

Intercession is more than specific:
it is pondered. It requires us to bear on our heart
the burden of those for whom we pray.
—GEORGE BUTTRICK

When we are linked by the power of prayer,
we, as it were, hold each other's hand as we walk
side by side along a slippery path; and thus by the
bounteous disposition of charity, it comes about that
the harder each one leans on the other, the more
firmly we are riveted together in brotherly love.
—GREGORY THE GREAT

In intercession you bring the person,
or the circumstance, that impinges on you
before God until you are moved by His attitude
towards that person or circumstance.
—OSWALD CHAMBERS

If we truly love people, we will
desire for them far more than it is within our
power to give them, and this will lead us to prayer.
Intercession is a way of loving others.
—RICHARD FOSTER

There is nothing that makes us love a man
so much as praying for him.
—WILLIAM LAW

*Knowing that intercessory prayer is
our mightiest weapon and supreme call for
Christians today, I pleadingly urge our people
everywhere to pray....Let there be prayer at
sun-up, at noon day, at sundown, at midnight,
all through the day. Let us all pray for our
children, our youth, our aged, our pastors,
our homes. Let us pray for our churches.*

*Let us pray for ourselves, that we may
not lose the word "concern" out of our Christian
vocabulary. Let us pray for our nation. Let us pray
for those who have never known Jesus Christ and
redeeming love, for moral forces everywhere,
for our national leaders. Let prayer be our
passion. Let prayer be our practice.*
—ROBERT E. LEE

Lord,
do not allow me to get so wrapped up
in my own needs
That i forget the needs of others,
grant me your compassion to feel the hurts
of my brothers and sisters.
give me a clearer vision of your love for others
And let my act of praying become a channel
Through which your blessings may flow.
in the name of Him who was
the servant of all, i pray,
amen.

-7-

WHEN GOD
DOESN'T ANSWER

Sometimes we experience miraculous immediate answers to our prayers.

Other times, the answers unfold slowly like a flower in the spring.

And there are still other times when our prayers seem unheard—when we do not get what we have so passionately requested. All of us know the disappointment of fervent prayer that fails to produce the prayed-for result. It can be confusing and painful. It can cause us to doubt the efficacy of prayer, our relationship with God, or even His goodness. Unanswered prayer is one of the great troubling realities for all Christians.

But there is really no such thing as an unanswered prayer. Our prayers are always answered. God's ear is always attuned to our requests, but sometimes His answer is not the one we wanted.

There are three answers to prayer:
yes, no, and wait.
—UNKNOWN

Even Jesus had to deal with unanswered
prayer....For our sins, He suffered beneath
the burden of that unanswered prayer.
—ANDREW MURRAY

Prayer is request. The essence of request,
as distinct from compulsion, is that it may or
may not be granted. And if an infinitely wise
Being listens to the requests of finite and foolish
creatures, of course He will sometimes grant
and sometimes refuse them.
—C.S. LEWIS

He does not care to give anything
but His best, or that which will prepare for it.
Not many years may pass before you confess,
"Thou art a God who hears prayer, and gives
a better answer." You may come to see that
the desire of your deepest heart would have been
frustrated by having what seemed its embodiment
then. That God should as a loving Father listen,
hear, consider, and deal with the request after the
perfect tenderness of His heart, is to me enough;
for it is little that I should go without what I pray
for. If it be granted that any answer which did not
come of love, and was not for the final satisfaction
of him who prayed, would be unworthy of God;
that it is the part of love and knowledge to watch
over the wayward, ignorant child; then the
seemingly unanswered prayer begins to abate,
and a lovely hope and comfort takes its
place in the child-like soul. To hear is not
necessarily to attend to—sometimes as
necessarily to refuse.
—GEORGE MACDONALD

*Dear Brethren, you shall by no means
despise your prayer, as if it were in vain,
for I tell you of a truth that, before you have
uttered the words, the prayer is already recorded
in heaven; and you shall confidently expect from
God one of two things: either that your prayer
will be granted, or that, if it will not be granted,
the granting of it would not be good for you.*
—BERNARD OF CLAIRVAUX

Sometimes our prayers seem unanswered
because we are impatient, because we do not
realize that God's timetable is not always the
same as ours.

*Never was faithful prayer lost.
Some prayers have a longer voyage
than others, but then they return with
their richer lading at last, so that the praying
soul is a gainer by waiting for an answer.*
—WILLIAM GURNALL

Frequently the richest answers
are not the speediest....A prayer may
be all the longer on its voyage because it
is bringing us a heavier freight of blessing.
Delayed answers are not only trials of faith,
but they give us an opportunity of honoring
God by our steadfast confidence in Him
under apparent repulses.
—CHARLES SPURGEON

Other times we realize only in hindsight that the answer we had hoped for would not have been the best thing for us. God, in His wisdom and love, often withholds our requests on the grounds that they would be harmful to our ultimate good.

I have lived to thank God that
all of my prayers have not been answered.
—JEAN INGELOW

O sad estate
Of human wretchedness; so
weak is man,
so ignorant and blind, that
did not God
sometimes withhold in mercy
what we ask,
We should be ruined at our
own request.
—HANNAH MORE

We shall come one day
to a heaven where we shall
gratefully know that God's great
refusals were sometimes the true
answers to our truest prayer.
—P. T. FORSYTH

If God had granted all the
silly prayers I've made in my life,
where should I be now¿
—C. S. LEWIS

We pray for silver,
but God often gives us gold instead.
—MARTIN LUTHER

God is not mocked.
He does not answer prayers
if He has already given us the answer
and we are not willing to use it.
—WILLIAM MACDONALD

We, ignorant of ourselves,
Beg often our own harms,
which the wise powers
Deny us for our good;
so find we profit
By losing of our prayers.
—WILLIAM SHAKESPEARE

If it were the case that
whatever we ask God was pledged
to give, then I for one would never pray again,
because I would not have sufficient confidence
in my own wisdom to ask God for anything.
—J. A. MOTYER

When you ask, you do not receive,
because you ask with wrong motives,
that you may spend what you get
on your pleasures.
—JAMES 4:3

And we must always remember that even when we get what we prayed for that it is not automatically a spiritually healthy thing. Sometimes an answered prayer can be spiritually hazardous if it causes us to become proud of spiritual attainments or assume that our answer was generated because God is impressed by our spiritual state.

> *There are two main pitfalls on the*
> *road to mastering of the art of prayer.*
> *If a person gets what he asks for, his humility*
> *is in danger. If he fails to get what he asks for,*
> *he is apt to lose confidence. Indeed, no matter*
> *whether prayer seems to be succeeding or*
> *failing, humility and confidence are two*
> *virtues which are absolutely essential.*
> —A TRAPPIST MONK

Thank you, Father,
that in your wisdom you let many
of my prayers go "unanswered."
Because I cannot see into the future;
Because I cannot see into the hearts of others;
Because I so seldom know what it is
that I really need,
I trust in your wisdom.
Thank you for teaching me
that you are the ultimate answer
to all my prayers.
Amen.

-8-

TAKING UP THE CHALLENGE

The pages of this book have been filled with insights on prayer, testimonies of its effectiveness, and suggested methods that we might use to improve our prayer lives. Some of these methods and ideas might be new to you, and you may be excited about the prospect of putting them into practice. But if you approach the task with the expectation that the difficulties of prayer will be solved by learning a new technique or gaining a new perception, you will most likely be disappointed. Prayer is hard work. There is no easy shortcut to vibrant prayer.

Disappointment can also arise from thinking that every method will work for every person. But not every insight will be fruitful to every believer. Prayer is individual; as individual as your own personal relationship with God. What was helpful

to one of the great writers of the past may be inef-
fective, unworkable, or impractical for you, no
matter how much effort you expend. What is
inspiring and eye-opening to one may be confusing to another. God made each of us unique, and
His ways with us will be as individual as we are.

Find the way of prayer that works best for you.
Often the most natural way of praying will be the
best. For example, my knees tend to wear out
pretty quickly, so I have found that a bracing walk
outdoors creates, for me, a natural environment for
prayer. But just because it is natural or easy doesn't
necessarily mean it is the best path. After all, we
cannot allow ourselves to become lazy when it
comes to spiritual matters. It would be a mistake
to let your prayers be limited by your preferences
or your natural tendencies. It is a good thing to
break out of your accustomed mold. By the same
token, don't always be searching for some new
wrinkle or method. At its heart, prayer is a pretty
simple act. Don't muddy the waters by a search
for the novel or the offbeat.

One of the best ways to improve your prayer
life is by learning more about the focus of your

prayers: God. Read the Scriptures to gain greater understanding of who God is and what He has done for us. Let your thinking about life be shaped by biblical truths, and consequently, your prayers as well. Our prayer lives are often limited or thrown off course by poor theological understanding, but they can be set afire when we gain deeper understanding about God's ways. If we seek God with our minds as well as our hearts, new vistas of understanding will open before us and more focus will be given to our prayers.

As I look back over the pages of this book, I am reminded again of the relevance of the writings of the past for those of us who live in the present. There is much we can learn if we will bend our ears to the insights of the great saints who have preceded us. They challenge us anew not to take lightly the serious task of prayer.

But what should we do with the insights we have gained? If they remain only interesting concepts, if they do not penetrate into our hearts and challenge us, then they have failed to do their work. As Andrew Murray reminds us, prayer is something we learn by doing:

*Reading a book about prayer,
listening to lectures, and talking about it
is very good, but it won't teach you to pray.
You get nothing without exercise, without practice.
I might listen for a year to a professor of music
playing the most beautiful music, but that
won't teach me to play an instrument.*

Hopefully, the profound thoughts about prayer recorded in this book will help us make the choice to give ourselves to prayer, for prayer begins with a choice: We must choose to involve God in all the various aspects of our life. We won't really begin to make progress in prayer until we decide to take prayer seriously. We may need to do some rearranging of our prioritizing. Prayer should be one of the major priorities in the life of the believer. Sadly, it often is crowded out by the press of other activities, even our "religious" ones.

When we look into the lives of these great men and women of the past, we see a commitment to prayer. In fact, the strength and unflagging persistence of their prayer lives were such that they sometimes were referred to as the "athletes of prayer" or "prayer warriors." In the same way that an athlete will structure his or her life around the accomplishment of a desired athletic goal—running faster, hitting the ball farther, developing greater endurance, and so on—so did these athletes of prayer make prayer central to their lives. They expended themselves to become better, and more fervent, pray-ers. By doing so, they changed the world.

Are we willing to do the same? Are we willing to restructure our goals, our priorities, and our time around the act of serious prayer? Will we expend the necessary energy to work at becoming more focused in our prayers? Will we make times of prayer a central part of our schedule rather than something we do if we can find the extra time? Are we willing to keep on practicing, to keep on praying, even when it becomes difficult or boring, seems pointless, or seems too emotionally demanding?

All the rich and profound thoughts on prayer, which we have as a legacy from the past, are of no value to us unless they actually cause us to take prayer more seriously.

And we should take prayer seriously.

Any way we look at it, prayer is an awesome privilege. To think that the Creator of all things

desires to hear about all our needs and concerns is
a staggering thought. Seen from an eternal per-
spective, the matters that concern us are, for the
most part, rather trivial. Who are we that God
should bother to hear us? And yet, God does not
hold our concerns to be trivial. The wonder of it all
is that God is willing to concern Himself with
what concerns us. That He is willing, and in fact
desirous, to lend an ear to our problems and struggles reveals a great deal about our relationship
with Him and His love for us.

Love is God's motivation for giving us the gift of
prayer. It should also be our prime motivation in
praying. We do not pray primarily to receive whatever it is we think we need, or to fulfill what we
perceive to be our religious duty. We pray because
we love God. We pray because our hearts cry out
from their need to communicate with Him. We
pray because we desire His companionship with
us on the pathway of life.

God is not an impersonal metaphysical force or
an indifferent "supreme being." He has revealed
Himself to be a lover—one who wants to be in
relationship with His creatures. He is the source
of all life and the giver of every good gift, even

those gifts that may not seem good to us at the time we receive them. He is infinite, but He is also personal.

Prayer is the most intimate activity we can share with God. I do not think it is too much of a stretch to suggest that prayer is to our relationship with God what the sexual relationship is to a healthy marriage. It is the utmost in self-revelation, where we bare our hearts before God. In prayer we reveal our true selves and make ourselves vulnerable to God. We spend our passion in pursuing His pleasure. We long for His presence with us and in us.

As we undertake the life of prayer, then, it is important that we keep our eyes on what really matters. We should focus not on the methods of prayer, but on the One to whom we pray. A heart that pants for God as a deer pants for water (Psalm 42:1) is the foundation of true prayer. We pray because we long to be in communication with God. We want to speak, to pour out our hearts, to be heard. The glory of prayer is that we can be, in a sense, face to face with God, even as Adam was in the garden when God walked with him "in the cool of the day." Prayer truly is the pathway to the very heart of God!

FAMOUS PRAYERS AND
PRAYERS OF THE FAMOUS

Our prayers need not be beautifully articulated or theologically profound to receive an answer from God. He appreciates the honest outpourings of our heart. Our words are precious to Him. But, from those who have expressed themselves well in their praying, perhaps much more clearly than we are capable of ourselves, we can learn the discipline of thinking carefully and praying seriously.

*Come near to the holy men and women
of the past and you will soon feel the heat
of their desire after God. They mourned for Him,
they prayed and wrestled and sought for Him day
and night, in season and out, and when they
had found Him the finding was all the sweeter
for the long seeking.*
—A.W. TOZER

I have gathered together a collection of some well-known "written" prayers, many composed by the same writers whose thoughts on prayer we have considered.

We can use these prayers as models to fashion our own prayers, inspirations to prepare our hearts to pray, or ways to give voice to concerns and feelings that we cannot articulate. We can make these prayers our own, for sometimes they will help us to express what we struggle to put into words for ourselves. When prayed with focus and concentration they can give our hearts wings to fly upward to God.

I ask you, Lord Jesus,
To develop in me, Your lover,
an immeasurable urge towards You,
an affection that is unbounded,
a longing that is unrestrained,
a fervor that throws discretion to the winds!
The more worthwhile our love for You,
all the more pressing does it become.
Reason cannot hold it in check,
fear does not make it tremble,
wise judgment does not temper it.
—RICHARD ROLLE

O most merciful Redeemer, friend, and brother,
may we know Thee more clearly,
love Thee more dearly,
and follow Thee more nearly,
day by day. Amen.
—RICHARD OF CHICHESTER

I believe it! 'Tis Thou, God, that givest,
'tis I who receive,
In the first is the last, in thy will is
my power to believe.
All's one gift; thou canst grant it moreover,
as prompt my prayer
As I breathe out this breath,
as I open these arms to the air.
—ROBERT BROWNING

You, O Eternal Trinity, are a deep sea
into which, the more I enter, the more I find,
and the more I find, the more I seek. O abyss,
O eternal Godhead, O sea profound, what more
could You give me than Yourself? Amen.
—CATHERINE OF SIENA

O Lord my God,
thank You for bringing this day to a close;
thank You for giving me rest in body and soul.
Your hand has been over me and has guarded
and preserved me. Forgive my lack of faith and
any wrong I have done today, and help me to
forgive all who have wronged me. Let me sleep in
peace under your protection, and keep me from
the temptations of darkness. Into Your hands I
commend my loved ones and all who dwell in
this house; I commend to You my body and soul.
O God, Your holy name be praised.
Amen.

—DIETRICH BONHOEFFER

Brief Biographies of quoted writers

ABBA ANTHONY (c. 250–356) The first Christian monk, a hermit who withdrew to the Egyptian desert.

AUGUSTINE (345–430) Early African bishop and prolific writer.

HENRY WARD BEECHER (1813–1887) Early American preacher.

BERNARD OF CLAIRVAUX (1090–1153) Medieval spiritual leader and writer.

DIETRICH BONHOEFFER (1906–1945) German theologian and pastor, author of numerous books, martyred by the Nazis.

E. M. BOUNDS (1835–1913) Popular writer of many books on prayer.

PHILLIPS BROOKS (1835–1893) American minister and hymn writer.

ROBERT BROWNING (1812–1889) English poet.

GEORGE BUTTRICK (1892–1980) Anglo-American pastor and devotional writer.

JOHN CALVIN (1509–1564) French reformer and systematic theologian.

CATHERINE OF SIENA (1347–1380) Mystic, church leader.

OSWALD CHAMBERS (1874–1917) Scottish Bible teacher and writer.

JOHN CHRYSOSTOM (c. 345–407) Greek church father known as "golden mouth" for his oratorical skills.

JOHN CLIMACUS (579–649) Ascetic and mystical writer.

Philip Doddridge (1702–1751) English church leader and writer.

J. H. EVANS (1801–1846) English missionary to Canada.

FRANÇOIS FÉNELON (1651–1715) French mystical writer.

CHARLES G. FINNEY (1792–1875) American evangelist and writer.

P. T. FORSYTH (1848–1921) Scottish theologian and writer..

HARRY EMERSON FOSDICK (1878–1969) American Baptist minister and writer.

RICHARD FOSTER (1942–   ) American devotional writer.

FRANCIS DE SALES (1567–1622) Bishop of Geneva and mystical writer.

GREGORY THE GREAT (540–604) Influential church leader and pope.

O. HALLESBY (1879–1961) Norwegian theologian.

ABRAHAM HESCHEL (1907–1972) Orthodox Jewish theologian.

WILLIAM LAW (1686–1761) Cambridge don, clergyman, and author.

BROTHER LAWRENCE (c. 1605–1691) Monk and mystical writer.

ROBERT E. LEE (1807–1870) American confederate general.

C. S. LEWIS (1898–1963) English professor, prolific writer, and Christian apologist.

MARTIN LUTHER (1483–1546) German founder of the Reformation, author of numerous treatises, commentaries, and devotional books.

GEORGE MACDONALD (1824–1905) Scottish minister, novelist, and poet.

ROBERT MURRAY MCCHEYNE (1813–1843) Scottish minister.

HANNAH MORE (1745–1833) English writer and playwright.

G. CAMPBELL MORGAN (1863–1945) English preacher and Bible teacher.

GEORGE MUELLER (1805–1898) German philanthropist, founder of numerous orphanages in Britain.

ANDREW MURRAY (1828–1917) South African devotional writer.

ORIGEN (c. 185–254) Important early church theologian from Alexandria.

RICHARD OF CHICHESTER (1197–1253) English
  bishop.

RICHARD ROLLE (c. 1295–1349) English mystical
  writer.

J. C. RYLE (1816–1900) English bishop and writer.

BASILEA SCHLINK (1904–   ) German nun and
  devotional writer.

WILLIAM SHAKESPEARE (1564–1616) English play-
  write and poet.

CHARLES SPURGEON (1834–1892) Gifted English
  preacher and writer.

CORRIE TEN BOOM (1892–1983) Concentration
  camp survivor, writer, and speaker.

TERTULLIAN (c. 160–230) Early church theologian.

TIKHON OF ZADONSK (1866–1925) Russian church
  leader.

A. W. TOZER (1897–1963) American pastor and
  devotional writer.

WALTER WINK Contemporary American theologian.

Terry Glaspey is an editor and an author of several significant books, including *Your Child's Heart, Not a Tame Lion: The Spiritual Legacy of C. S. Lewis,* and *Great Books of the Christian Tradition*. He lives in Eugene Oregon.